Little Miss Dancey Pants

By: Kourtni Mason

Illustrated by: Sharad Kumar

AuthorHouse™
1663 Liberty Drive
Bloomington, IN 47403
www.authorhouse.com
Phone: 1-800-839-8640

Published by AuthorHouse 12/12/2014

ISBN: 978-1-4969-5678-1 (sc)
ISBN: 978-1-4969-5679-8 (e)

Library of Congress Control Number: 2014921641

My name is Addison . . . Madam Queen Busy Body! From a very young age, dance has been my favorite hobby.

I sing songs really loudly and bounce in my seat, while snapping my fingers and tapping my feet.

Mama says, "Oh, Addie! Sit still. You will wrinkle your dress."

But, I just can't seem to give it a rest.

I skip and move and bounce and shake. The joy I feel I just can't fake.

I don't care who's watching, I prance and prance. Boys tease, "Look, it's Little Miss Dancey Pants!"

But, I was born this way. I've known dance for so long, because Mama's a ballerina - graceful and strong.

She sways across the floor, leaps to the sky, and turns on one leg in the blink of an eye.

I will follow in Mama's footsteps. This I know to be true, which means that one day, I'll surely be a beautiful dancer, too.

Saturday is my favorite day of the week, because I get to travel to the studio and watch Mama on her feet.

One day, Mama saw me in the corner trying to follow her moves. I did not have them all, but I certainly had the groove.

She asked, "What are you doing Miss Dancey Pants?" I said, "I want to be just like you. I just want to dance."

So, Mama turned up the music and led me to the floor. As soon as I started moving, she could say no more.

The next day Mama enrolled me in my very first class. I was so nervous waiting for the time to pass.

My teacher, Ms. Dianne, greeted me with a great big hug. She introduced me to everyone, including Karrington, my best bud.

The dancers took ballet, tap and jazz together. Each day
I was there I had the best time ever!!

Before long, Ms. Dianne named Karrington and me the "Dancers of the Week." I couldn't wait to tell Mama. She'd be so proud of me.

When it was time for our recital, we wore pretty pink
tutus with gloves and a bow. I was so excited. I even had
a solo!

Mama and Daddy were smiling from ear to ear when I took my place.

As I performed my solo, the light shined brightly on my face.

I knew it was meant to be. For I was a beautiful dancer
you see.

When the recital was over, the dancers went to greet our fans. I spotted Mama and Daddy and ran to Daddy's outstretched hands.

Eagerly I asked, "Did you see?! Did you see?!" He beamed with pride and said, "You were as beautiful as can be."

And Mama replied, "You're a dancer now, Addie. Just like me!"

But, I knew it all along. I laughed and skipped while holding their hands. Of course I'm a dancer . . .

I'm little Miss Dancey Pants!

CPSIA information can be obtained at www.ICGtesting.com
Printed in the USA
BVOW10s2027221214

380536BV00006B/10/P